MW01028456

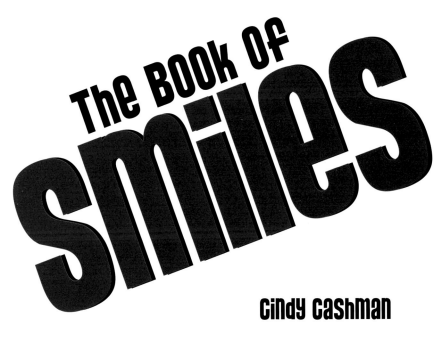

The BOOK OF smiles

Cindy Cashman

**Andrews McMeel
Publishing**

Kansas City

Photo and illustration credits

Corbis/Bettmann: pp. 11, 12, 14, 25, 27, 29, 30, 39, 40, 42–43, 44, 46–47,
    49, 59, 63, 65, 68, 70
The Library of Congress: pp. 21, 33, 60
Photoalto: pp. 6, 34, 36, 66
p. 4, Todd Wolfson; p. 50, Gabriela Mendez; p. 52, Bobbi Colorado; pp. 55
    and 74, Preston Palmer; p. 73, Duke University
p. 22, Smile on a Stick® © copyright 1990 The Bauer Group, Inc.

03 04 05 06 07 WKT 10 9 8 7 6 5 4 3 2 1

ISBN: 0-7407-3531-4

Library of Congress Control Number: 2002117425

To my three favorite people,
who make me smile and laugh:
my mother, Donna Kress;
my son, Erick Nelson;
and my sister, Sandy Cashman Palmer.

introduction

There's just something about a smile. You see someone with a big goofy smile, or even the faintest hint of a grin, on his or her face and you can't help but smile back; a smile is something you always want to return to sender. It doesn't matter who's smiling, either—your best friend, your spouse, a baby, a dog, the supermarket cashier, a movie star— a smile is infectious in the nicest way.

Best of all, a smile is 100 percent natural. Babies smile almost from birth. Infants (even some as young as two days old) tend to smile at faces. By the time they are one year old, babies are able to recognize the important people in their lives, and many have a special smile for these individuals. And smiling is not necessarily something we learn by imitation. According to Frank McAndrews, psychology professor at Knox College in Galesburg, Illinois, babies who can't see smile just like everyone else. It seems our faces were made to smile.

Given the choice between a person with a big smile or someone scowling over in the corner, who are you most likely to be drawn to? Join the smiling faces here and treat yourself to a feel-good smilefest!

A smile is . . .

free and easy.

5

Life is short,
but a smile
takes barely
a second.

—Cuban Proverb

A smile is a *curve* that sets everything straight.

—Phyllis Diller

8

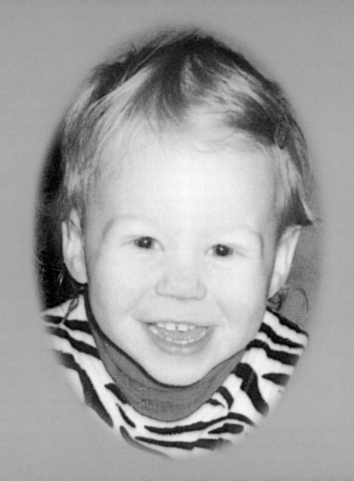

smile,

it's free therapy.

—DOUG HORTON

Wrinkles should merely indicate
where smiles have been.

—mark twain

13

A SMILE costs nothing, but gives much.
It enriches those who receive,
without making poorer those who give.
It takes but a moment, but the memory
of it sometimes lasts forever.
None is so rich or mighty that he can
get along without it, and none is so poor
but that he can be made rich by it.

—Rabbi Samson Raphael Hirsch

15

Smiling is contagious—you catch it like the flu;
When someone smiled at me today, I started
    smiling too.
I passed around the corner, and someone saw my
    grin;
When he smiled, I realized I'd passed it on to him.

I thought about that smile, then I realized its
    worth;
A single smile, just like mine, could travel round
    the earth.
So, if you feel a smile begin, don't leave it
    undetected—
Let's start an epidemic quick and get the world
    infected!!!

—anonymous

17

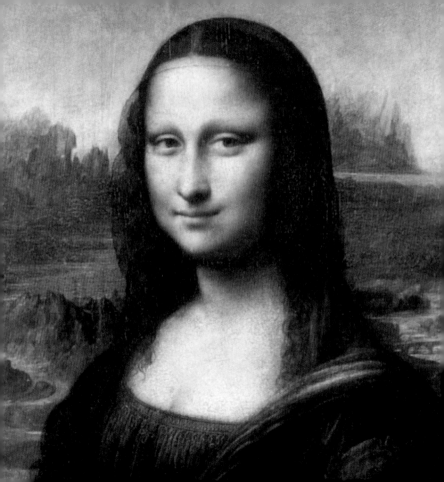

A smile can . . .

charm or disarm.

19

Smile: It makes people wonder
what you are thinking.

—anonymous

20

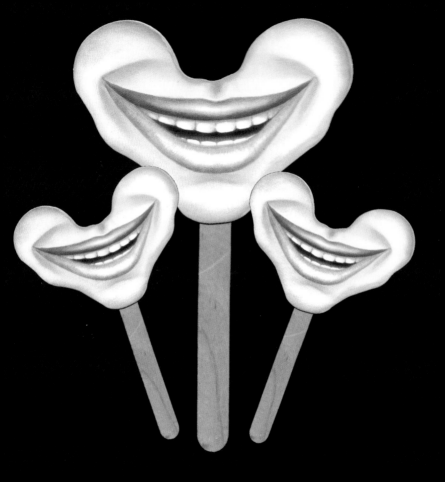

a person

without a

smiling face

must not

open a shop.

—chinese proverb

What the people need is a way to make them smile.

—The Doobie Brothers

24

Let a **smile** be your umbrella.

—Irving Kahal, Francis Wheeler, and Sammy Fain

(from *Give My Regards to Broadway*)

Better by far you should forget and smile
Than that you should remember and be sad.

—Christina Georgina Rossetti

(from "Remember")

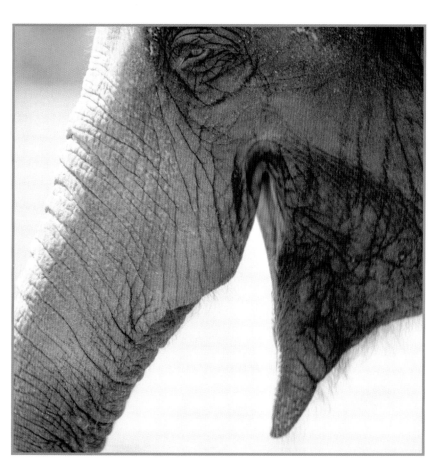

A smile can . . .

Start or strengthen a friendship.

The World is like a mirror, you see?

Smile, and your friends smile back.

—Japanese saying

33

Let us always meet
each other with a smile,
for the smile is the
beginning of love.

—mother Teresa

35

What SUNSHINE is to flowers,
SMILES are to humanity.

These are but trifles, to be sure;
but, scattered along life's pathway,
the good they do is inconceivable.

—JOSEPH ADDISON

Wear a smile and have friends,
wear a scowl and have wrinkles.

What do we live for if not to make
the world less difficult for each other?

—George Eliot

38

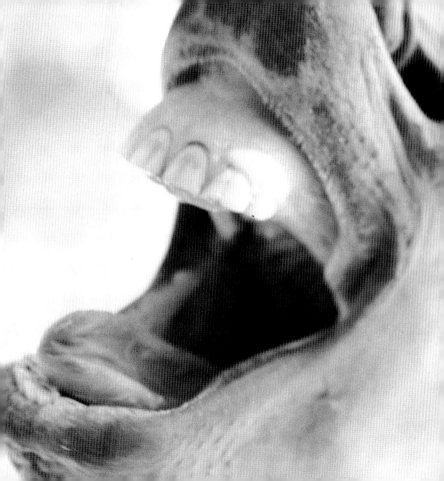

a winning smile makes winners of us all.

—source unknown

41

a smile can . . .

bring families together.

42

Smile at each other, smile at your wife, smile at your husband, smile at your children, smile at each other—it doesn't matter who it is—and that will help you to grow up in greater love for each other.

—Mother Teresa

A smile can . . .

start a relationship
or seduce a lover.

She gave me a smile
i could feel
in my hip pocket.

—raymond chandler

(from *Farewell, My Lovely*)

never frown
because you
never know
who might be
falling
in love
with your
smile.

—justine milton

51

Smile: It's the second best thing one can do with one's lips.

—anonymous

A smile is the
light in the window
that lets people
know you're at home.

—anonymous

54

How to Smile When You Don't Feel Like Smiling

Hang around with happy people.

Watch funny movies.

Play with a child under five.

Let a dog kiss you on the lips.

Print out a smiley face and tape it onto your own face.

Push up either side of your mouth with your fingers.

Call someone you love on the phone.

Read silly cards at the supermarket.

Take a smiley friend to lunch.

Think of a happy memory.

a smile
makes you
look better
on the
outside and feel
better on
the inside.

58

You're never fully dressed without a smile!

—Martin Charnin and Charles Strouse

(from *Annie*)

a smile is a frown turned upside down.

—anonymous

If you're not
using your smile,
you're like a man
with a million dollars
in the bank and
no checkbook.

—Les Giblin

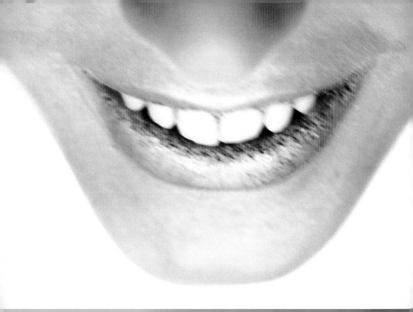

It takes **seventeen muscles** to smile and **forty★three** to frown.

—anonymous

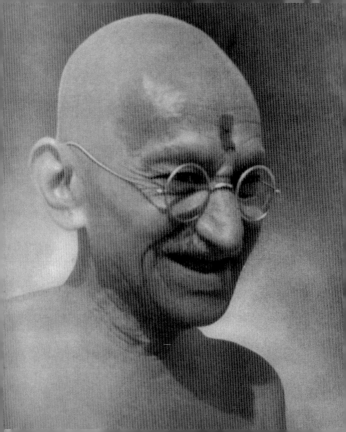

Now and then one sees a face
          which has kept its smile pure and
undefiled. Such a smile transfigures;
          such a smile, if the artful but know it,
is the greatest weapon a face can have.

—Helen Hunt Jackson

69

it is easy enough to be pleasant,
When life flows by like a song,
But the man worth while is the one
    who will smile,
When everything goes dead wrong.

—Ella Wheeler Wilcox
(from "Worth While")

71

A smile creates happiness in the home,
fosters goodwill in business, and is the countersign
of friendship. It brings rest to the weary, cheer to
the discouraged, sunshine to the sad, and is nature's
best antidote for trouble. Yet it cannot be bought,
begged, borrowed, or stolen, for it is something
that is of no value to anyone until it is given away.
Some people are too tired to give you a smile.
Give them one of yours, as none needs a smile
so much as he who has no more to give.

—rabbi samson raphael hirsch

Smiles
Jerome H.
Remick & Co.
Detroit
New York
Words by
J. Will Callahan
Music by
Lee S. Roberts

Too often we underestimate
the power of a touch, a smile,
a kind word, a listening ear,
an honest compliment,
or the smallest act of caring,
all of which have the potential
to turn a life around.

—LEO BUSCAGLIA

75

If you have a favorite smile picture or funny photo that you think belongs in a follow-up to this book, please send your photo to:

Cindy Cashman
c/o Andrews McMeel Publishing
4520 Main Street
Kansas City, Missouri 64111

(Photos will not be returned.)

Or you can e-mail your photo to photos@cindycashman.com or visit www.cindycashman.com.

By sending us your photo you are giving us permission to use it in a future book.